JOYFUL NOISE!

A Service for the Celebration of Easter

RUTHANNE KELCHNER-COCHRAN

C.S.S. Publishing Co., Inc.

Lima, Ohio

JOYFUL NOISE!

9027 / ISBN 1-55673-213-9   PRINTED IN U.S.A.

The Resurrection of Our Lord (II)
John 20:1-18

The women went their way with herbs and spices,
There to anoint his body in the tomb.
Their hearts were torn by memories of crisis
Their thoughts were full of sorrow, dread and gloom.

For Friday had been such a day of sorrow
As they had followed Jesus to the hill,
Where on the cross, his promise of tomorrow
Was crucified. And death had drunk its fill.

And now, as they drew near to where they'd laid him,
In a borrowed tomb and placed a rock before,
They wondered how they'd reach the grave they'd made him
And roll away the stone before the door.

But lo! the grave was open; the stone was rolled away.
And when they stooped to enter, they found no body there.
The wrapping cloths were lying where once his body lay.
But he whom they were seeking was not there anywhere.

Two men were standing there. Or were they angels?
Their robes were white and glistened like the sun.
And when they saw that fear had struck the damsels,
They spoke as though the two of them were one.

"Why seek ye here among the dead, the living?
Remember what he said in Galilee,
That men would seek his death without forgiving,
But after death, the grave would set him free."

The women then remembered Jesus' saying
And went to the apostles on the run.
The men dismissed the tale they were conveying.
But they'd believe before the day was done.

We celebrate that day begun in sadness
And with a mournful visit to the grave
Because it turned about with hopeful gladness.
And faith in God's abiding pow'r to save.

Reprinted from *A Gospel Treasury, Cycle C* by Andrew Daughters. (Poems based on Lectionary Gospels.)

3

Narrator: Now on the first day of the week Mary Magdalene came to the tomb, while it was still early, while it was still dark, and saw that the stone had been taken away from the tomb. So she ran, and went to Simon Peter and the other disciple, the one whom Jesus loved, and said to them,

Mary: "They have taken the Lord out of the tomb, and we do not know where they have laid him."

Narrator: Peter then came out with the other disciple, and they went toward the tomb. They both ran, but the other disciple outran Peter and reached the tomb first; and stooping to look in, he saw the linen cloths lying, but he did not go in. Then Peter went into the tomb and saw the linen cloths lying also, and the napkin, which had been on his head, not lying with the linen cloths but rolled up in a place by itself. The other disciple, who reached the tomb first, also went in, and he saw and believed; for as yet they did not know the scripture, that he must rise from the dead. Then the disciples went back to their homes.

But Mary stood weeping outside the tomb, and as she wept she stooped to look into the tomb; and she saw two angels in white, sitting where the body of Jesus had lain, one at the head and one at the feet. They said to her,

Angels: "Woman, why are you weeping?"

Mary: Because they have taken away my Lord, and I do not know where they have laid him."

Narrator: Saying this, she turned round and saw Jesus standing, but she did not know that it was Jesus. Jesus said to her,

Jesus: "Woman, why are you weeping? Whom do you seek?"

Narrator: Supposing him to be the gardener, she said to him,

Mary: "Sir, if you have carried him away, tell me where you have laid him and I will take him away."

Jesus: "Mary."

Mary: "Rabboni!"

Jesus: "Do not hold me, for I have not yet ascended to the Father; but go to my brethren and say to them, I am ascending to my Father and your Father, to my God and your God."

Narrator: Mary Magdalene went and said to the disciples,

Mary: "I have seen the Lord.'

Narrator: And she told them that he had said these things to her.

4

Production Notes

Explanation of the Service

This Easter service is designed to be used in the outdoors, in the Sanctuary, or any place conducive to worship. Easter is a joyous time for the Christian. This service is a celebration of Easter joy.

A cross, which may be used during the Lenten Season, is placed in the middle of the worship center. (A cross made from the wood of the Christmas tree is particularly meaningful. The Christmas tree is symbolic of life. The cross is a symbol of the living Christ. Without Christmas, and the birth of Jesus Christ , we could not have Easter which is the Resurrection of Jesus Christ over death. The birth, the death, and the risen power of Jesus *is* Christianity.) On the top of the cross is placed a Crown of Thorns. The rest of the cross is decorated with dogwood and lilies. You may wish to print the legend of the dogwood tree in your bulletin.

> *The dogwood was the tree which was used as the Cross for Christ. Jesus, sensing the pain of the dogwood said, "Your strength which has shamed you shall not remain, but in slender grace you will bear beautiful flowers of spring, and your blossoms formed in the shape of the Cross shall not be the symbol of sorrow and loss, but of the joy my resurrection shall bring."*

The white lily with its trumpet-shaped flower represents new life and new beginnings.

Music

Organ, choirs, hand bells, trumpets, or a brass quartet may be used for the service. Use instruments with the hymns.

The Gathering of the People

Outside Service: Trumpets or a brass quartet play Easter voluntaries as the people gather for worship. The musicians move to different areas, so the music may be heard in different dimensions of sound.

Indoor Service: Trumpets or a brass quartet play outside the church, moving around the building, and playing from different locations. Also, the musicians could be in the Narthex, or in hallways around the Sanctuary.

The Trumpet or Brass Call to Worship

Any Bach Chorale would be suitable. The Chorale should be played giving an echo effect. The musicians are in different areas. One musician is very close to the worshiping congregation, one between the other two, and the last trumpet sound comes from a distance.

The Choral Introit

This is sung by a soloist, combined choirs, or one choir from the back of the worshiping area.

Musical Selections for Hand Bells, Choirs, or Soloist

"I Know My Redeemer Liveth"   Handel
"I Live"   Rich Cook
(*Heart Warming Sacred Favorites*, Vol. 2, Benson Publishing Co.)
"Alleluja! Alleluja!"   Mozart
"I Walked Today Where Jesus Walked"   (Meaningful for outside service.)

"The Easter Song"   Anne Herring
"Because He Lives"   William J. Gaither
"His Name Lives On"   Roger L. Horne
(*Heart Warming Sacred Favorites*, Vol. 2, Benson Publishing Co.)

Hymns

"Christ The Lord Is Risen Today" with Trumpet descant by
    Paul Sjolund. (*Hymns For The Family Of God*)
"Because He Lives"   Gloria and William
                                         Gaither
   (*PRAISE — Our Songs and Hymns*)
"He's Living Today"
   (*PRAISE — Our Songs and Hymns*)
"Up From The Grave He Arose"   Robert Lowry
"Rise Again"   Dallas Holm
   (*PRAISE — Our Songs and Hymns*)
"He Lives, He Lives"   Ackely

The Scripture Readings

The Gospel
The Gospel is read by a narrator and persons speaking for
Mary, Mary Magdalene, the Angel, and Christ. The scripture
is acted out in a very simple manner.

Outside Area: An area which can be used to represent a
garden. Actors are in simple costumes of that time. Jesus
wears a plain white garment.

Sanctuary Area: The area of the Altar can be used, with Jesus
standing among the actors.

The Response to the Scriptures

Choral Response: "Joy To The World" (*Verse One*) or
                     "He Lives, He Lives" (*Chorus*)

The Closing of the Service

The Hymn of Triumph

Outside: During the singing of this hymn the person acting as Christ appears at a far distance with arms stretched forward. If there is a hill or a mountain in the area, the person should stand on a high point which is visible to the worshiping fellowship.

Inside: During the singing of the hymn the person acting as Christ appears in the front of the Sanctuary with arms stretched forward. Jesus pauses for a brief time, then continues to walk down the aisle.

The Choral Response

Suggestions:

"Joy To The World" (*Verse Four*)
"He Lives, He Lives" (*Chorus*)
"Threefold Amen"
"Alleluia, Alleluia" Traditional (*Hymns For The Family Of God*)

(Please note: the writer of this service uses "Joy To The World" because it is a very dynamic hymn which expresses the true meaning of both the Easter and Christmas Seasons.)

The Sacrament of Holy Communion
Holy Communion may be celebrated following the Easter Meditation, using the procedures of the local congregation.

Suggested Themes and Texts
"I Have Good News For You"	1 Corinthians 15:57
"Easter! Either . . . Or"	John 20:19
"What Did You Expect?"	Luke 24:34
"A Joyous Surprise!"	Matthew 28:6
"Does Easter Make A Difference To You?"	John 14:19
"Only An Idle Tale! . . . Or Is It Truth?"	Luke 24:10, 11

JOYFUL NOISE!

A Service for
the Celebration
of Easter

The Service

The Gathering of the People

The Trumpet Call to Worship
    "The Son Of God Has Come"   J. S. Bach

The Choral Introit
    "Morning Has Broken" (*Verse One*) Bumessan

The Call to Worship

Minister:	In the name of the risen Christ, our Lord and Savior, I greet you. Let our celebration of victory through the Cross begin reverently, but joyously.
	Have you heard the Good News? Christ, the Lord has risen from the grave!
People or Congregation:	*Alleluia! Alleluia! The Lord, our God, is alive!*
Minister:	Come, celebrate the Living Christ!
People:	*He has done great things.*
Minister:	He has brought Life that never ends.
People:	*For me to live is Christ.*
Together:	*JOY TO THE WORLD — CHRIST IS RISEN! ALLELUIA! HE LIVES! ALLELUIA! ALLELUIA! AMEN!*

The Hymn of Victory "Christ The Lord Is Risen Today"

11

The Invocation (*In Unison*)

O God, we rejoice with great joy as we come together to recall the Resurrection of Jesus Christ, Your Son, our Savior, and our Redeemer. Our morning song is filled with praise and thanksgiving, for the tomb is empty. May the celebration of this hour fill our hearts with Christ's gift of love, so we may live the glorious message of Easter; in Christ we have a new life which is eternal. Thanks be to the Living Christ. Amen

The Musical Selection

The Holy Scriptures

The Old Testament Lesson   *Psalm 150*

Minister: Hallelujah! Yes, praise the Lord!

Men: *Praise him in his temple, and in the Heavens he made with his mighty power.*

Women: *Praise him for his mighty works. Praise his unequaled greatness.*

All: *Praise him with the trumpet, and with the lute, and the harp.*

Men: *Praise him with the drums and dancing.*

Women: *Praise him with stringed instruments and horns.*

Men: *Praise him with the cymbals, yes, loud clanging cymbals.*

Minister: Let everything alive give praises to the Lord! You praise him.

All: *Hallelujah!*

The Epistle   *1 Corinthians 15:51-58*

The Gospel   *John 20:1-18*

The Response to the Scripture

Minister: The joyous news of our salvation: Jesus is not dead. He lives!

People: *Thanks be to God. Christ lives, and so do I!*

The Choral Response to the Scripture
"Joy To The World" (*Verse One*)

The Easter Prayer (The Lord's Prayer)

The Giving of Our Gifts

The Offertory

The Doxology

The Prayer of Dedication (*In Unison*)

O God, in the joyous spirit of this day, we bring these gifts of love. Accept our offering, and bless it, so that it may be used to tell others of the Good News: that Christ has victoriously conquered death and because he lives, life shall be eternal for all who believe in him. Amen

The Musical Selection or The Hymn of Preparation

The Easter Meditation

The Hymn of Triumph "He Lives! He Lives!" Ackley

The Passing of the Easter Peace

Greeting:
  The joy of this morning be yours
Response:
  May it fill your heart and life, also.

The Easter Benediction

  Minister: The joy of the Good News that Jesus
         Christ lives is your gift today.

  People: The hope of this Easter message fills
        our lives and our hearts.

  Minister: The love of the risen Lord be yours
         now and forever.

  Together: HALLELUJAH! AMEN! AMEN!

The Choral Response "Joy To The World" (*Verse Four*)

The Postlude   "Thine Is The Glory"
               (*Trumpets and Organ*)

How Close Dare You Come? 20:1-9

Need: There is something scary about death. We tend to keep our distance from a corpse or grave. We proceed with all caution when we tread on unfamiliar or dangerous ground. On the first Easter, three people come to the tomb with three different approaches. How much are we like them?

Outline: How close are you to the Easter tomb?

a. A distant position — Mary Magdalene.

She saw from a distance that the stone was rolled away. Assuming that the body was stolen, she rushes to tell Peter and John. We can take the same position — look at the Resurrection from afar: doubt, misunderstanding of the Resurrection, non-involvement.

b. A close position — John.

John stood at the opening of the tomb but was afraid to enter. He looked into the tomb, but he was too timid to enter by himself. In our time, we get close to the resurrected Christ, but we do not enter into Christ. We are content to be spectators of the drama.

c. A direct position — Peter.

Impulsive, daring, brazen Peter rushed into the tomb. He is not afraid to enter where angels may fear to tread. He sees the absence of Jesus' body, the grave clothes, and the facial napkin. But, the evidence does not lead him to believe Jesus has risen. His bravado is fruitless. Only timid John, now in the tomb, senses the meaning of the evidence and believes.

Notes taken from *Lectionary Preaching Workbook, Series A* by John R. Brokhoff, page 126, no. 3.

God's Order

1 Corinthians 15:20-26, v. 23: Each, however, in his own turn: Christ rose first; then when Christ comes back, all his people will become alive again.

Object: A set of cards with numbers on them from one to ten, or a variety of numbers that the children can put in order.

Good morning, boys and girls. A very happy Easter to you. The best day of the whole church year is here and we can all celebrate together. Jesus Christ is risen today! He is not dead but alive! They did all of the things they wanted to do to him, including the worst of all — crucifixion — and today he is alive! The people in the Bible shouted, "Hallelujah, Hallelujah, Christ is risen from the dead." Isn't that a joyous sound? We should do that ourselves. Let's all say it together. "Hallelujah, Hallelujah, Christ is risen from the dead!" Doesn't that make your heart jump and your feet feel like running? I know that it is the way I feel.

But what does this mean for you and me? Why should we be so happy that Jesus is alive, and they could not kill him? *(Let them answer.)* I'll tell you why. We are going to live again, too, just as Jesus did. Did you know that? Well, it's true. Let me show you what I mean.

I have some cards with numbers written on them. I am going to lay them down and I want you to put them in the right order. *(Take out the cards and read the numbers in a very mixed up order.)* Now, I want you to start with the smallest number and put them in a line until the last one is the largest number. *(Allow them a few seconds to do this.)* There is a certain order that is right and it would not work any other way.

The same thing is true about the idea that the first one to come back to life after he died was to be Jesus. Now the Bible says that there will be one more thing happen before other people who die shall come back to life. This other thing is that Jesus must return to earth again, and when he comes back all of the people who believe in him will also be brought back to life. That is the order God has set. There is only one way, just as there is only one way to arrange the numbers.

Just think, part of it has already happened. Jesus is risen from the dead. Now all we are waiting for is for him to come back to earth as he promised. Then we will all be taken with him to a wonderful place that we call heaven or God's Eternal Kingdom. It is nice to know that God works in a good order so that we can count on him and know what there is to expect. If you can put numbers in order, you can also know what the order is that God has made for us to join Jesus in heaven.

Children Sermon excerpt — *Pass It On* by Wesley T. Runk, C.S.S. Publishing Co.